ROGER CARSWELL

Things God wants us to know

Publishing
a division of 10ofthose.com

Copyright © 2022 by Roger Carswell

First published in Great Britain in 2007

British Library Cataloguing in Publication Data
A record for this book is available from the British Library

ISBN: 978-1-914966-91-0

Designed and typeset by Pete Barnsley (CreativeHoot.com)

Printed in Denmark

10Publishing, a division of 10ofthose.com
Unit C, Tomlinson Road, Leyland, PR25 2DY, England

Email: info@10ofthose.com
Website: www.10ofthose.com

1 3 5 7 10 8 6 4 2

Contents

1.

Questioning our questions

'Atheism never composed a symphony. Never painted a masterpiece. Never dispelled a fear. Never healed a disease. Never gave peace of mind. Never dried a tear. Never established philanthropy. Never gave an intelligent answer to the vast mystery of the universe. Never gave meaning to man's life on earth. Never built a just and peaceful world. Never built a great and enduring civilisation.' – Charles M. Houser

On a number of occasions I have enjoyed sitting with friends, tucking into food and grappling with issues raised when we have started with the question, 'If you could ask God anything, what would it be?' It's a great discussion starter. Sometimes the topics raised are deeply personal, whilst others are quite straightforward, though genuinely felt, questions of belief. The response, though, is never dull.

There is a Middle Eastern proverb that says, 'It is more difficult to ask a good question than it is to give a good answer'. You just have to listen to a toddler and it is clear that naturally human beings ask questions, and want answers. It is how we learn. Sadly, there is a danger in our busy world that we simply live by rote. If our leisure time is consumed by soaps, soccer and stardom then there is a danger that we will cease to question anything! Could it be that some of the issues that concern us are not those highest on God's agenda? Perhaps we are missing the point even when we ask questions; so, are we thinking through the right questions? Supposing we were to ask God what He wants us to know, how would He respond? If God is there, is He silent, or does He communicate? And if He does speak, what does He want to communicate to us? What is He passionate about? What is on the mind of God? Is what concerns Him, the same as what bothers us?

Douglas Coupland's book *Life after God*, which was published in 1994, caused quite a stir. He concludes it by saying:

Now – here is my secret:

I tell it to you with an openness of heart that I doubt I shall ever achieve again, so I pray that you are in a quiet room as you hear these words. My secret is that I need

God – that I am sick and can no longer make it alone. I need God to help me give, because I no longer seem to be capable of giving; to help me be kind, as I no longer seem capable of kindness; to help me love, as I seem beyond being able to love.

That's quite an honest admission! Christians have good reason to believe that God *is*, and that neither Douglas Coupland nor anyone else need be left in a frustrating quandary. God has not just wound up the world like a toy, and left it so that with curiosity He can watch it unwind. Rather, He is interested, involved, and even *in* the world that He has made. God is concerned and communicates.

I would like to get into the mindset of art gallery security officers! When I have half a chance, I pop into galleries and am left in awe at the amazing, accurate and artistic beauty created by strokes of a brush, pen or knife, and portrayed on canvas. I could stare for ages, yet I notice the security guards sitting apparently bored and disinterested. Is that how they are supposed to be? Are they paid to look indifferent, to bite their finger nails and gaze into space? Or have they become desensitised to the value and beauty that hangs yards away from them? Likewise, I fear that many brought up in the Western countries may similarly have lost the wonder and awe of God's world and the good news of Jesus. Familiarity may have bred contempt, or at least disinterest. However, to those willing to look, there are treasures, that God wants us to know are worth discovering.

It is fundamental to the Christian message that God has revealed Himself to the world He has made. We are often given the impression by the media that human beings are on a long search for God. Sometimes educationalists convey the idea that God is on top of a mountain, and people are making their way to Him using different routes, but all going in the same direction. These may be intriguing ideas, but they are far from the God who has made Himself known.

Christians believe that the Bible is God's message to humanity; that when we open it to read, we are in effect opening the mouth of God and allowing Him to speak to us. The Bible makes it clear that men and women are not actually looking for God, but rather running away from Him. We are wanting to do our own thing.

God has made Himself known in various ways. The world and the universe around us are wonderful. As we will see, all of creation has been ruined; but there is still something magnificent about the world in which we live. Whether it is the infinitesimally minute DNA structure that makes us as humans, or the enormity of space and the billions of stars, there is evidence of design, and therefore a designer. To gaze through either a microscope or a telescope provides evidence that there is order, intricacy and design to all that we see. To pause and look at a delicate snowdrop which pushes itself through the hard frozen winter soil, or to wonder at a beautiful sunset, is a reminder that God is infinite in His creativity, orderly in His design, and extravagant in His provision. That is why, contrary to what is often thought, so many great scientists of the past and present had or have a robust Christian faith.

However, God has not only shown us that He exists, but also what He is like. He has done this through the Bible, and through the man Jesus. As well, God has been at work in history, and the lives of individual men and women, making people aware of Him, and bringing people into a personal relationship with Him.

So God has not left us in the lurch, groping in the dark to try to find truth, as the media would have us believe. He wants us to know ultimate reality; He has no desire for us to fumble through life, existing but blinkered or blinded to spiritual truth. God wants us to know about Him, and actually to know Him.

The nineteenth-century poet, Elizabeth Barrett Browning's parents disapproved so strongly of her marriage to Robert that they disowned her. Almost weekly, Elizabeth wrote love letters to her mother and father, longing for everything to be sorted out between them. They never once replied. After ten years of letter writing, Elizabeth received a huge box in the mail. She opened it. To her dismay and heartbreak, the box contained all of her letters to her parents. Not one of them had ever been opened.

Today those love letters are among the most beautiful in classical English literature. Had her parents opened and read only a few of them reconciliation might have been effected. Similarly, God has spoken to us, making Himself known to the people He has made. Sadly, what He has said is often neglected or even rejected. God is there; He is not silent, but in practice He can be silenced if we refuse to listen. It is easy to do, in effect, what Elizabeth Browning's parents did, and throw God's love and message back in His face.

If we are open to God, we will find that He disturbs our presuppositions. Throughout our lives we are bombarded with our secular age's attitudes to life. Living in a post-Christian era we pick up attitudes that are antagonistic to the world view that God has made known to us. God is marginalised; conveniently kept at a distance; only to be consulted in times of trouble. We will find that God's agenda can be quite different from that of the government, the media or even our peers. It is amazing what we accept without ever really questioning. Jesus confronts the beliefs and behaviour, which are contrary to what is right, and that can be disturbing. As we read the Bible, we will probably find that what it says is quite different from the view of the Bible that we were taught in Religious Education lessons years ago. It is a thrilling and exciting book, making God known to us, and focusing attention on Jesus Christ. Just the realisation through reading, that the Bible is not religious thoughts of human beings of long ago, but God vibrantly speaking to us today, is overwhelming.

God's priorities are very different from our materialistic, pleasure-seeking society. But then our society offers little to those who are wondering what is the purpose of life, or to those who are grieving because they have messed up their lives, or to those who have lost a loved one, or to those who are considering what happens when a person dies. The Bible does not dodge the straightforward questions of where have we come from, why are we here and where are we going. There are answers to these issues.

We discover these answers as we look at some of the themes of the Bible, examining what God wants us to know about Himself, and about ourselves. The restlessness and emptiness, which often characterise our lives, need not be the norm. In finding answers to life's biggest questions, there is freedom and joy to be discovered.

In the Book of Proverbs in the Bible, there is a chapter where wisdom, which is the knowledge of God, is portrayed as a woman prophet preaching in places where people gather in the city. She is drawing attention to herself, like a wayward woman, but making a very different kind of offer with her encouraging invitation:

'Now then, my sons, listen to me; blessed are those who keep my ways. Listen to my instruction and be wise; do not ignore it. Blessed is the man who listens to me, watching daily at my doors, waiting at my doorway. For whoever finds me finds life and receives favour from the Lord. But whoever fails to find me harms himself; all who hate me love death.'[1]

---

1   Proverbs 8:32-36, see also 1:21-22

2

God wants us to know
who He is

'Who can look upon statues or paintings without thinking at once of a sculptor or painter? ... And when one enters a well-ordered city ... what else will he suppose but that this city is directed by good rulers? So he who comes to the truly Great City, this world, and beholds hills and plains teeming with animals and plants, ... the yearly seasons passing into each other, ... and the whole firmament revolving in rhythmic order, must he not ... gain the conception of the Maker and Father and Ruler also?'[2] – Philo (1st century, Jewish writer)

It is common to hear people say words like, 'My view of God is...' The problem with that sentence is that there could be six billion views of God, and they could all be

---

2   Philo: Special Laws, i. 6

wrong! The issue is not what is my view of God, but what is God's view of God? What is He really like? What has he told us about Himself?

There are others who believe that they themselves are god! The trouble with that idea is that the gods will never live up to expectations, and will die when they die! This is hardly a god worthy of worship, trust or service!

Of course, there are those who don't believe in God at all. The atheist, Richard Dawkins, expressed his nonbelief by describing an evolved world of 'no design, no purpose, no evil and no good, nothing but blind, pitiless indifference'.[3] But those words don't ring true and jar against what we know of ourselves. There are too many unanswered questions in Dawkins. He doesn't explain the scores of fulfilled prophecies in the Bible, nor the historical evidence for the resurrection of Jesus, or how we know what is good or bad, or the dramatic change of life that a person who trusts Jesus experiences.

There is a deep-seated conscious awareness of something 'other' in each of us, and our hearts are restless until they find their rest in God. The people I meet instinctively know that life has a purpose. That awareness is reinforced when they witness the birth of a baby; no father, seeing a little son or daughter emerge

---

3   *River out of Eden* published by Weidenfeld and Nicolson, 1995, p. 133

into the world cries, 'That's a wonderful conglomeration of chance chemicals!' Equally, to gather around a grave to witness the burial of a loved one reminds us of the meaningfulness of life. (Who ever muttered at such a scene, 'Well there goes a meaningless existence where nothing of value was achieved'?). Are we really to believe that by chance something impersonal came about, and that with time it developed the things that made him/her personal, such as love, significance, hope, purpose, reasoning, beauty and a sense of right or wrong? To rob humanity of its awareness of being made in the image of God is identity fraud![4]

Try telling a mother in Africa who is striving to eke out a living for her children that there is no real meaning to life. Or try explaining to someone who has been falsely imprisoned that there never will be ultimate justice. Or try comforting parents who have just buried their little child by saying that there is no life after death. Deep down we know the atheists are wrong because God has put within us all an awareness of Him our Maker, and has gone to great lengths to reveal Himself to the world He made.

Confusion about God is sometimes caused because different religions have their own beliefs as to what their

---

4 Geoff Chapman, 'Answers in Genesis' prayer news, October – December, 2005. www.answersingenesis.org/qa

god is like. It is politically correct to say that they are all valid but their beliefs can be mutually contradictory. For example, Muslims and Jews believe in one God, Hindus have millions of gods, and Buddhists have no God. Clearly, not every religion can be true, or even helpful to the person who wants to find out about God. Religions tell us to do certain things, to be certain types of people and to adhere to certain dogmas. In contrast, Christianity says that doing and being and even adhering are not what does the trick. In fact there isn't a trick to be done! Rather there is a relationship with God to be gained, and that is established by receiving what God has been and done for us. Rather than adhering, we are encouraged to trust; to rest in what God is offering to us.

God has revealed Himself to the world that He has made. He has done so in many ways, as we will see. He wants us to know who He is and what He is like. Open the Bible anywhere, and as you read it will become apparent that God is making Himself known to us. Some of what we find is familiar. For example, we read that 'God is love'. Yet, those famous three words are revolutionary to the people who live in anguish that their god is spiteful and vindictive, needing to be pacified. Other aspects of God might be beyond our comprehension, e.g. that God is eternal, and has no beginning and never ends. But if we could understand all there was to know about almighty

God, either God would not be God or we would not be human. To read the Bible is in effect to open the lips of God and allow Him to speak to us.[5]

Now let us see what God has revealed about who He is.

First, *God is eternal* (He has no beginning and no end) and He is timeless (bigger than time and beyond time). Of course, our finite minds cannot fathom the depths of this because everything we know has a beginning and an end. C.S. Lewis answered questions that this might arouse arguing, 'It is clear that there never was a time when nothing existed; otherwise nothing would exist now.'[6] God has revealed Himself saying He is from everlasting to everlasting:[7] a thousand years are like a day in God's sight.[8] *God is spirit.*[9] It is not possible, therefore, to put God in a display cabinet or scientific laboratory to scientifically analyse Him, for He cannot be seen or touched. Nevertheless, He is 'He', not in a masculine way but in a personal sense. God is a real person who, like the people He made, has emotion and senses. God can be known

---

5 There is significant evidence that the Bible is God's message to humanity. Elsewhere I have summarised some of the reason why Christians believe that the Bible is God's Word. See *Why believe?* by Roger Carswell, published by Authentic Media, 1990, chapter 1, 'Why believe the Bible is the Word of God'

6 *Miracles* by C.S. Lewis, published by Macmillan, 1960. Ch. 11, p. 88

7 Psalm 41:13 & Isaiah 40:28

8 2 Peter 3:8

9 John 4:24

and enjoyed, so human beings can have a relationship with Him. He wants to be our Heavenly Father, and make us His children.

There is only one God.[10] This is made absolutely clear throughout the Bible, as God wants to steer His people away from the multiplicity of false gods and idols that the nations round about were worshipping. There is, though, multiple personality in the Godhead, so that we read of the Father, the Son and the Holy Spirit each being God. There is only one God who is in three persons. There is love, communication, submission and personality within the triune God. We will see that God is love. For that to be true there must be multiple personality within the person of God: how else would God's love have been expressed before there was anything created? In 'eternity past' the Father loved the Son, who loved the Holy Spirit, who loved the Father. There has always been love within the Godhead.

God is all-powerful.[11] He is the one who spoke and formed the universe out of nothing, bringing everything into being. It is hard for us to take in the vastness of the universe. Cambridge physicist Stephen Hawking says in his best-selling *A Brief History of Time* that our galaxy is

---

10 Deuteronomy 6:4; Mark 12:29

11 Revelation 19:6

an average-sized spiral galaxy that looks to other galaxies like a swirl in a pastry roll and that it is over 100,000 light years across – about six hundred trillion miles. He says, 'We now know that our galaxy is only one of some hundred thousand million that can be seen using modern telescopes, each galaxy itself containing some hundred thousand million stars'. It is commonly held that the average distance between these hundred thousand million galaxies (each six hundred trillion miles across and containing one hundred thousand million stars) is three million light-years! It is noteworthy that Charles Darwin himself in his autobiography and his letters, as an old man, repeatedly remarked, 'I cannot believe with my mind that all this was produced by chance.'

God is the Creator,[12] and not the creation of peoples' imagination. The idea that if there weren't a God we would have to invent one is nonsense. If there wasn't a God we would not be here to invent one! The world we inhabit must have had an origin. That origin must have consisted in a cause. That cause must have been intelligent. That intelligence must have been supreme, and that which was and is supreme we know by the name God. The Creator of the world is the owner of it. He keeps the world going, by His power, and has a purpose for all He has made.

---

12 Genesis 1:1

God knows all things.[13] He understands us better than we understand ourselves. He is never surprised by anything, for the past, present and future are all known to Him. He has never thought, 'I didn't expect that!' There is never an emergency cabinet meeting in heaven, for He is never caught out unawares. He knows all the details of our lives. He weighs our secret thoughts. He knows the motives of our actions and all the machinations of our minds. He hears people using the breath that He gave them to argue against God, and He laughs at them.[14]

God is everywhere,[15] so it is impossible to hide from or escape His presence. There is no such thing as a Godforsaken spot on earth. God is infinite and is not limited by time, energy or capability.

God never changes.[16] He does not have moods. He is consistent and reliable. When He gives His word, He can be relied upon; He is trustworthy. God is eternal, without beginning or end; he cannot die.

God is totally pure and spotless.[17] Such holiness not only means that God has done no wrong or is incapable of wrong, but that He is intrinsically pure. There are angels

---

13 Psalm 147:4

14 Psalm 2:4

15 Psalm 139:7

16 Numbers 23:19; James 1:7

17 Isaiah 6:3

in heaven, who themselves have never sinned, but who when entering the presence of God are over-awed by the sense of His absolute holiness.

God has never grown accustomed to wrongdoing; He has never 'learned' to tolerate wrongdoing, but consistently hates sin, ungodliness and unrighteousness. He cannot excuse or overlook what is wrong, because He knows better than anyone the destruction that sin causes. He does not sit round a negotiating table compromising on what is or is not acceptable.

His standards are absolute. He is not the God of situational ethics, adjusting what is permissible according to the fads or trends of the times! Of course, if there were no God, then there could be no absolute standard of right and wrong. We might judge that the common good was an acceptable framework, but who is to determine what is good? I remember, as a teenager seeing on the news, the atheistic Communist leader Khrushchev sitting at his desk in the United Nations pounding it with his shoe and shouting, 'It's wrong! It's wrong!' What a strange and inconsistent thing for an atheist to say!

Injustice is infuriating. God is absolutely just,[18] and is concerned for equity and justice. There is no partiality or unfairness in Him, so when God ultimately judges, He

---

18 Proverbs 24:12

will judge all people according to truth. God cannot be hoodwinked; He knows all the evidence, so the judge of all the earth will always do what is right. Sin must be punished, for He cannot merely overlook wrongdoing as if it does not matter. He is truth, and all that is contrary to it is against Him.

And *God is love*.[19] His love is infinite and eternal; yet His love is focused on each individual. When God loves, He loves the world; when God gives, He gives His Son; and when God saves, He saves forever, for we read in the Bible, 'For God so loved the world that He gave His one and only Son, that whoever believes in Him should not perish, but have eternal life.'[20] God is not unmerciful, but delights in showing mercy, compassion and forgiveness to all who will turn to Him. His love is greater than friendship, or charitable love, or romantic love. They can be passionate and strong, but they can also fade and fail, whereas God's love is consistent. He loves us even when we don't love Him; He is patient. We read of Him, 'But you, O Lord, are a compassionate and gracious God, slow to anger, abounding in love and faithfulness.[21]

---

19 1 John 4:16

20 John 3:16

21 Psalm 86:15

God came into the world in the person of Jesus.[22] It was the plan of God, even before the foundation of the world, that, at the right moment, He the Creator would become like us His creation. God had no intention of turning His back on, or washing His hands of, the world He had made and loved. God would take on Himself flesh and blood. He would enter our world, coming to rescue the very people who had turned from Him and gone their own way.

The Bible explains this as 'The Father sent His Son to be the Saviour of the world.' [23] Or as a child expressed it, 'Jesus is God with skin on!' The sixteenth-century German reformer Martin Luther understood that for Jesus to accomplish all that He did, He had to be God Himself. Luther wrote: 'Now, to give grace, peace, everlasting life, forgiveness of sins, to justify, to save, to deliver from death and hell, surely these are not the works of any creature, but of the sole majesty of God ... We must think of no other God than Christ.'[24]

Some years ago, a few days before Christmas, I joined a team of people from a Glasgow church who go on a late night 'soup run' each Thursday. It was very cold. We

---

22 John 1:1 and 14; Isaiah 9:7

23 1 John 4:14

24 *Martin Luther: Righteous Faith* by Drew Blankman. Published by IVP, 2002, pp. 57 & 58

set off at 10 p.m. and visited hostels, people living rough on the streets and under flyovers, as well as those who work the streets through the night. We gave them each a hot drink, soup, sandwiches and a Christmas present. A businessman, called William,[25] led the team. For over fifteen years he had not missed a single Thursday night to be involved in the work.

Just after 3 a.m. we found a drunk lying on some grating near a department store. William went up to him, shook him and said, 'Jock, it's William. I have food for you.' Jock did not respond. Eventually William lay on the damp ground next to Jock, spoke face to face with the man, gave him some hot chocolate, and put the present and sandwiches in Jock's overcoat pocket.

To me, it was a thumbnail picture not only of the Christmas message, but the Christian message. God could have ignored us, in much the same way that William could have chosen to stay at home each week. Instead, God, in the person of Jesus Christ, came into this world 'to seek and to save those who are lost.' Sadly, Jock was too drunk to take much notice of William's care and kindness.

God is still at work in our world today; He communicates and is not silent. He has revealed Himself to the world that belongs to Him. The Holy Spirit is active: He holds

---

25 Name changed for anonymity

back the world from its perilous rush to wickedness; He points people to a realistic view of themselves, and then to see Jesus as the one who can forgive and change them not only for time, but also for eternity.

Nothing could be more important than getting things right concerning God. To mistake who God is has consequences that affect the way we spend our lives, and even our eternity. There is no reason to make a mistake, because God has made Himself abundantly clear.

I recently found myself sitting opposite a nineteen-year-old-girl whilst travelling from the north of Scotland by train to Yorkshire. We soon got into conversation and she told me her story. She comes from a broken home, but is now living with a forty-year old woman. In many ways, my heart went out to the girl who had drawn such a bad deal in life. I told her about myself, and how it was I had come to know God. The questions and answers flowed as we cheerily chatted around all sorts of subjects. Eventually I gave her a copy of the Gospel of John from the Bible. She sat and read it from cover to cover, occasionally making comments like 'this is real' or 'I never knew the Bible was so interesting,' and 'All we ever got taught in R.E. at school was about other religions, not Jesus'. God speaks, and He will speak to any individual who is open to Him, through His written message to humanity, the Bible.

3

God wants us to know
who we are

'God defend me from ever looking at a man as an animal.' [26]
– Ralph Waldo Emerson

We may be infinitesimally minute compared with the size of the universe, but human beings are fearfully and wonderfully made.[27] Just as there is a sense of awe about the vastness of space, so there is inevitable wonder at the detail of the microscopically small DNA structure or the human cell. The way we human beings hold together and function is magnificent.

There is clear evidence that we have been designed, and therefore, there must be a designer. For example,

---

26 *The Book of Unusual Quotations*, edited by Rudolf Flesch, Cassell, 1959
27 Psalm 139:4

think for a moment of our nervous system. Inside us are some 100,000 miles of nerve fibres along which messages shoot at speeds of 300 miles per hour. Or think of our DNA, which contains about 2,000 genes per chromosome – 1.8 metres of DNA are folded into each cell nucleus. A nucleus is six microns long. This is like putting thirty miles of fishing line into a cherry pip. And it isn't simply stuffed in. It is folded in. If folded one way, the cell becomes a skin cell. If another way, a liver cell, and so forth. To write out the information in one cell would take 300 volumes, each volume 500 pages thick. The human body contains enough DNA that, if it were stretched out, it would circle the sun 260 times![28] The delicacy and intricacy with which we have been woven together demonstrates that we are not here by blind chance or accident, but have been made for a purpose, and therefore have meaning.

Each human being is special, and of immense value. I was saddened when I read in a newspaper[29] of an Australian woman, Alexia Harriton aged twenty-four, who is deaf, blind and physically and mentally disabled, wanting to sue the doctor who allowed her to be born. Her mother said that if she had known the extent of Alexia's disabilities she would have had an abortion. One

---

28 Information from Dr. John Medina, genetic engineer, University of Washington, in 1995 lecture at Multnomah Bible College, Portland, Oregon

29 *Daily Telegraph* 11/11/2005

sympathises hugely with both Alexia and her mother, and yet still there is a dignity and significance about human life. The Bible expresses the awe about the wonder of the world around, and human beings in particular:

When I consider Your heavens,
the work of Your fingers,
the moon and the stars,
which You have set in place,
what is man that You are mindful of him,
the son of man that You care for him?
You made him a little lower than the heavenly beings
and crowned him with glory and honour.
You made him ruler over the works of Your hands;
You put everything under his feet ...[30]

Human beings have been created. At the very beginning of the Bible we have the drama of how God brought all things into being. The creation of the first man and woman was the ultimate in creation, and God delighted in what He had formed. We were made that we might know and enjoy God forever. We were made in the image of the triune God. Human beings are physical creatures. We have different colours, features, shapes and sizes, all

---

30 Psalm 8:3-6

of which make people so interesting. Just the masses of photographs in print the world over, which portray faces, demonstrates how fascinating we are to each other.

But we are not merely physical creatures. We are more than bodies. We each have personality, or the soul, so that we are distinctive characters with a variety of gifts and abilities that form a fascinating kaleidoscope of energetic humanity.

However, what makes humans unique in the world is that we also have a spirit. We were made to know, appreciate, enjoy and have a relationship with God who made us. The Bible speaks about 'the whole spirit, soul and body'[31] of people, and as it states it, the spirit of a person comes first and is the most important part of our being. True humanity is about us walking in companionship with God, at one with Him in the purposes He has for the world and us.

Human beings were created with an eternal existence. Though there is a fascination with the trivia, there is an eternal dimension to humanity, which makes us ask big questions as to who we are, what we are doing and where we are going. Because the relationship with God we are created to have has been broken, we can easily feel insecure as to important truths God wants us to rest in. Henry

---

31 1 Thessalonians 5:22

Bowler expressed them in an 1855 painting. He portrayed a widow in her twenties leaning against a newly dug grave near to a germinating chestnut tree. Engraved on the tombstone are the words of Jesus, 'I am the resurrection and the life.' Bowler's title for the painting is, *The doubt: 'Can these dry bones live?'* Yet there are repeated assurances in the Bible, as well as the natural, rational sense in each of us, that this life here on earth is not all there is.

We read in the Bible, 'Multitudes who sleep in the dust of the earth will awake: some to everlasting life, others to shame and everlasting contempt.'[32] It is sometimes said that nobody came back from the dead to tell us about life after death. But Jesus died, and came back. It was He who spoke most of all about heaven and hell; 'Then they will go away to eternal punishment, but the righteous to eternal life,'[33] and 'I am the Living One; I was dead, and behold I am alive for ever and ever! And I hold the keys of death and Hades (Hell).'[34] The apostle Paul spoke of Jesus, saying 'Our Saviour, Christ Jesus, who has destroyed death and has brought life and immortality to light through the gospel.'[35] Each individual has an everlasting existence. It is strange then, that we are so time and earth bound that

32 Daniel 12:2

33 Matthew 25:46

34 Revelation 1:18

35 2 Timothy 1:10

we forget that there is more to life than all we touch and see now. George Orwell once described how a wasp was sucking jam on some buttered bread on a plate. Orwell cut the wasp in half. The wasp paid no attention, but merely went on with its meal. In fact, Orwell described how the jam poured from its severed oesophagus! Only when it tried to fly away did it realise the dreadful thing that had happened to it! Human beings can be rather like the wasp, but when the time comes to 'fly away' there will be an awful realisation of the wrong priorities that have characterised so many. We are made to last forever. We will never pass our sell-by date.

The spirit, soul and body of a person together make a living being. There is inter-twining and communication between the three distinctives that make up a human being.

The greatest tragedy to hit the world occurred when the first human beings, instead of enjoying all that God had given them, rebelled against Him. They dared to defy God and shake their fist in His face refusing to accept His rule over creation. They wanted to know both evil and good, even though it would cost them dearly. The open defiance brought into the world devastation and ruin.

The close relationship between God and humans was broken, so God appeared distant to them. Sin, suffering and death would characterise what was once a truly wonderful world. Hospitals, hearses and handkerchiefs (to wipe away tears) became the norm. Men and women died spiritually, so that God seemed distant. It is as if we have been given a certificate of divorce: once there had been a happy relationship, but now there is separation and awkwardness. Eventually each individual would die in spirit, soul and body. Men and women, who had been created by God, would be cut off from Him.

The American author Mark Twain was touring Europe with his young daughter. Everywhere royalty, well-known artists and scientists honoured him. He had red-carpet treatment. Near the end of the journey, his daughter said, 'Papa, you know everyone except God, don't you?' Ouch! It is probably also true of most of us!

Ever since that disastrous moment, individuals have been born with an inherited nature that does wrong. Theologians describe this as 'original sin'. It is the nature within us that leads us to do wrong. There is something majestic about each human, but we have been wrecked by the bias to do wrong.

The early twentieth-century actress Mae West in her inimitable way expressed this when she said, 'I used to be snow white, but I drifted.'[36] Actually, neither she nor we were snow white, but from the start are conceived with a nature that will lead us to do wrong. We don't have to

---

36 Taken from an Icon card (www.icon-art.com)

teach little children to tell lies, lose their temper, and be selfish or mean: they do them by nature. And the seed of sin within us sends its roots and shoots through every part of us so that we are permeated by wrongdoing. We naturally find ourselves breaking God's commandments. We neither love God with all our heart, mind, soul and strength, nor do we love others as we love ourselves. Yet Jesus said that these two commands were the summary of the Ten Commandments.

The result is that even the most respectable people are flawed; everyone is guilty of 'moments of madness'. From time to time we read of people who have laboured hard throughout their life to build themselves a good reputation and accumulate formidable skills, only to squander them over an evil obsession or an act of folly. We are all guilty before God.

Robert Louis Stevenson said, 'We all have thoughts that would shame even hell.' The Bible is even more straightforward: it says, 'There is none righteous, no not one', and 'All men are liars' and 'All have sinned and fall short of the glory of God'. In our weaker moments, we try to blame others, or our background, environment or events, but there comes a point when we have to accept the responsibility for our own wrong.

Human beings have become puzzling paradoxes, grasping after spirituality, and yet hoping to hide from God, at the same time.

This is not something to dismiss with a wry smile. In the Bible, we have four biographies or Gospels of Jesus: Matthew (which looks at Jesus as the King), Mark (which focuses on Jesus as a servant), Luke (seeing Jesus as the Saviour) and John (which concentrates on Jesus as the Son of God). It is in John's Gospel that we read,

For God did not send His Son into the world to condemn the world, but to save the world through Him. Whoever believes in Him is not condemned, but whoever does not believe stands condemned already because He has not believed in the name of God's only Son. This is the verdict: Light has come into the world, but men loved darkness instead of light because their deeds were evil.[37]

It isn't comfortable reading, but it is clear that we could not be in a more serious situation.

The apostle Paul was a brilliant and deeply religious Jewish scholar at the time of Jesus. He was disciplined and devout in his religious duties. As Christianity started spreading, after the death and resurrection of Jesus, Paul

---

37 John 3:17-19

was bitterly opposed to this new religion. Zealously, and bitterly, he persecuted the followers of Jesus until his dramatic conversion to Jesus Christ on the road to Damascus.[38] Later, it was Paul who wrote much of our New Testament part of the Bible (that part of the Bible written after Jesus' life, death, resurrection and ascension back to heaven). He wrote to Christians in the city of Rome, which he had not at that time visited, and he clearly explained the gospel message to them in the great book we call 'Romans'. In the book he explains that God cannot simply wink at the sin in the lives of people. Paul, who knew how to write in a gripping way, did not easily repeat himself, but in this letter he speaks of God's wrath against sin eight times.[39]

We need to be made right with God, so that the condemnation that is ours might be removed from us. Jesus came to do this for us. We didn't ask Him to, but He did so out of sheer love for us.

---

38 See Acts 9

39 Romans 1:18; 2:5, 8; 3:5; 4:15; 5:9; 9:22 and 12:19

4

God wants us to know
what He has done

'It costs God nothing, so far as we know, to create nice things; but to convert rebellious wills cost Him crucifixion.'[40] – C. S. Lewis

God has not made the world and left it to its own devices. Rather, He is passionate about all that He has created, and wants us to know what He has done. He wants us to enter into the joy of knowing Him, which He has gone to infinite lengths to bring about. Similarly, Christian people want others to know what God has done for them. I heard the story of a minister of a church who made an appointment to meet the editor of his local newspaper. Ushered into the executive suite, the minister introduced the reason for

---

40 *Mere Christianity* by C.S. Lewis, published by MacMillan, 1952, p. 179

the visit by saying, 'Sir, I am here to ask you to become a Christian!' The editor walked to a window overlooking the city that the newspaper served. Standing, he paused silently for some time, then turned and said, 'Thank you for your concern. Since I was a young boy at my mother's knee not a single relation or business associate has ever taken an interest in my soul.' God is interested in the soul, and in every aspect of each individual.

The master theme of the Bible is the unfolding drama of how God would devise means whereby we, who should be banished from His presence, could be drawn back into a relationship with Him. The focus is on Jesus Christ.

The Bible first of all looks forward to His coming, then describes it, and after that applies what Jesus has done to the church, the world and individual Christians. The apostle Paul, who wrote much of our New Testament, explained Jesus' mission. As far as he was concerned, it is as if Jesus came into the world to do just three days' work. It commenced when He was nailed to the cross, and culminated when He rose again from the dead. Paul rarely or never discussed the life of Jesus. There is little mention of Jesus' virgin birth, His temptations or miracles, His sermons, or His agonising prayer in the Garden of Gethsemene prior to His crucifixion. Jesus Christ came primarily not to preach the gospel, but that there might be a gospel to preach!

The four Gospels in the New Testament describe Jesus' amazing birth, life, ministry and teaching. To read Matthew, Mark, Luke and John is to allow Jesus to introduce Himself to us. It is as if He walks off the pages of the Bible, and invites us to meet Him.

Matthew and Luke tell us the Christmas story of Jesus' birth in the manger in Bethlehem. Though it is all too familiar in the West, it is such an enchanting story: the stable scene because there was no room in the inn, the angels announcing to shepherds the birth of 'the Saviour who is Christ the Lord' and their response, 'Let us go to Bethlehem and see this thing that has happened, which the Lord has told us about.' Then there is the visit of the wise men from the east, bringing gifts with them, and Herod's genocide against the babies of Bethlehem.

Its appeal as a story aside, its significance is that God was entering our world. The Creator was becoming like us, His creation. The opening of John's Gospel reads, 'In the beginning was the Word, and the Word was with God, and the Word was God …The Word became flesh and made His dwelling among us.'[41]

At Christmas, a junior school in Barnsley, South Yorkshire, was having a traditional school nativity play. Old people and parents had gathered into the school hall.

---

41 John 1:1 and 14

Everything was going well until the wise men appeared all dressed up in their dressing gowns and tinfoil crowns. The first two had said their lines, moved across stage and presented to the doll in the manger the gold and then the frankincense. However, when the third wise man with his gift of myrrh noticed his parents in the audience, his mouth fell open, and over-awed, he forgot his lines! At least he had sufficient presence of mind to keep moving. Slowly, the boy knelt by the manger to present his gift, but he could not remember what to say. The teacher in the wings whispered, 'Say something.' Still no words came. 'Say anything' the teacher said in desperation. The young actor looked in the manger, and then in a broad Yorkshire accent, said the only words he knew to say to a baby: 'Eeh, he's just like his dad!' The audience roared with laughter, but the boy was absolutely right. The baby Jesus born in Bethlehem is, as the Bible puts it, the image of the invisible God.[42]

God was big enough to become small, and strong enough to become weak. God, whom the heavens cannot contain, clothed Himself with humanity. He took on Himself flesh and bones and blood. Without laying aside His deity, God became a man. He was born of the virgin Mary; born of both humanity and deity. Jesus is fully

---

42 Colossians 1:15

God – as much God as God is God; and fully human – as much man as man is man. He is the God-man. He is not just God indwelling a man; there have been plenty of examples of such people. Jesus is not a man deified; such men are in the realm of myths and pagan systems of thought. Jesus is both God and man, combining in one personality the two natures.

Jesus (the name means 'Saviour') came into the world to reconcile us to God. 'For God was pleased to have all His fullness dwell in Him, and through Him to reconcile to Himself all things, whether things on earth or things in heaven, by making peace through His blood, shed on the cross.'[43]

After twenty centuries, Jesus remains the greatest man in history. Born in poverty and obscurity, as a youngster He was taken as a refugee to become an asylum seeker in Egypt. He received no formal education and worked as a labourer. He never wrote a book, or a song. Jesus formally preached and ministered for only three years, without travelling far. He never spoke to flatter the authorities, and refused to compromise His message to please His audience.

In those three years of public work, He made blind people see, the mute He enabled to speak, the deaf He

---

43 Colossians 1:19-20

made to hear, and He healed lepers and lame people. On two occasions He fed thousands of hungry people with a few loaves and fishes. He spoke to and calmed in an instant the rough storm at sea. He walked on water, dispelling the fear of terrified fishermen. Jesus Christ gave dignity to women, respect to the disabled, significance to children, credibility to the family and status to each individual. He called Himself 'the Friend of sinners' and forgave people their sins saying, 'the Son of Man has authority on earth to forgive sins'.[44] Explaining this statement Jesus said, 'It is not the healthy who need a doctor, but the sick. I have not come to call the righteous, but sinners.'[45]

Nobody spoke as Jesus did: He had authority. He gave to the world the highest moral standard, preaching only what He practised. So when Jesus commanded that we should love our enemies, do good to those who hate us, bless those who curse us, pray for those who ill-treat us, turn the other cheek or go the extra mile, He was telling us to do what He Himself had been living out. His word and His works never contradicted each other. There is no sham, spin or hypocrisy about what Jesus said. His teaching and His life have never been surpassed.

---

44 Mark 2:10

45 Mark 2:17

It is impossible to fault the life of Jesus. Judas Iscariot, the disciple who sold Jesus for thirty pieces of silver, the price of a slave, tragically committed suicide crying, 'I have betrayed innocent blood.' Pontius Pilate, the governor who ordered Jesus to be crucified, tried to appease the crowd who were braying for Jesus' death, by asking, 'Why? What evil has He done? I find no fault with Him.' The criminal crucified next to Jesus said of Him, 'This man has done nothing wrong.' And the Roman soldier responsible for ensuring Jesus really was dead, said, 'Surely this man was the Son of God'. Jesus' disciple Peter, who was always an activist said of Him, 'He *did* no sin;' John, who was very close to Jesus, said '*In* Him was no sin;' the great intellect Paul said, 'He *knew* no sin' and elsewhere we read, 'He was *without* sin.'

Throughout the time of Jesus' public teaching, He spoke saying that He would be crucified. It was the purpose of God the Father, Son and Holy Spirit that, at just the right moment in history, Jesus would come to this earth to go to the cross to deal with sin. This had been prophesied throughout the Old Testament, as prophets anticipated the coming Christ's death. The King of Israel, David writing 1,000 years before Jesus,[46] and the

---

46 See Psalm 22

prophet Isaiah[47] give a detailed description of how the suffering servant would carry on Himself the sin of the world. Isaiah wrote:

> *Surely He took up our infirmities and carried our sorrows, yet we considered Him stricken by God, smitten by Him, and afflicted. But He was pierced for our transgressions, He was crushed for our iniquities; the punishment that brought us peace was upon Him, and by His wounds we are healed. We all, like sheep, have gone astray, each of us has turned to his own way; and the Lord has laid on Him the iniquity of us all. He was oppressed and afflicted, yet He did not open His mouth; He was led like a lamb to the slaughter, and as a sheep before her shearers is silent, so He did not open His mouth.*[48]

C.S. Lewis was the professor of Medieval English Literature at Cambridge University. He was converted to Christ from atheism, whilst at Oxford, and is famed for writing the children's Narnia books. Whatever C.S. Lewis' intentions in writing *The Lion, the Witch and the Wardrobe*, he drew a similarity between Aslan, who is a lion, and Jesus.

---

47 See Isaiah 53

48 Isaiah 53:4-7

The land of Narnia was a land of winter, but it was never Christmas. That was until the majestic lion, Aslan, allowed himself to be slain, and then to rise again. When Susan, one of the children in the book, understood about the lion she was shocked and asked, 'Is he – quite safe?' The answer is very apt:

> *Mr. Beaver tells her more: 'Safe? ... Who said anything about safe? Course he isn't safe. But he is good. He's the King, I tell you.'*

The good King Jesus was taken and stripped naked before being beaten and humiliated. He was treated unfairly in a series of mock trials, and sentenced to be executed by crucifixion, even though his judge could find no fault in Him. He was crucified between two thieves. In the hours of terrible suffering, Jesus carried on Himself the sin of the world, the purpose of His coming to earth. Jesus came to pay the penalty of the wrong of which we are guilty. He, the eternal Son of God, took the weight of the sin of the world on Himself. Jesus Himself said, 'The Son of Man came not to be served, but to serve and to give His life a ransom for many.' The disciple of Jesus, Peter, as an old man, wrote letters to Christians scattered throughout the world saturating all he said with references to the cross of Jesus.[49] He said, 'For Christ died for sinners once and for all, the righteous for the unrighteous, to bring us to God. He was put to death in the body but made alive by the Spirit.'[50] John, the youngest of Jesus' twelve disciples wrote, 'The blood of Jesus (God's) Son, purifies us from all sin.'[51] And the apostle Paul wrote, 'You see, at just the right time, when we were still powerless, Christ died for the ungodly … But God demonstrates His own love for us in this: While we were still sinners, Christ died for us.'[52]

I remember once looking out of a university window into a bustling London street. Traffic wardens seemed very busy and I pondered on how a car driver could go through life without ever having to pay a parking fine. There were two possibilities. Either you make sure that you never park wrongly. However, that seems an impossible task for most, and certainly for me! There will always be an occasion when a mistake is made resulting in the parking ticket being attached to the windscreen. The other way is to find somebody who is willing to pay your fines in your place! If that sounds too good to be true, it is only an illustration of what Jesus has done for us. He has

---

49 1 Peter 1:2; 1:11; 1:19; 2:7; 2:21 and 24; 3:18; 4:1; 4:13 and 5:1

50 1 Peter 3:18

51 1 John 1:7

52 Romans 5:6 and 8

paid the price, satisfying the justice of God, whilst out of love for us Jesus carried our sins on Himself.

To enjoy a right relationship with God, who is absolutely righteous, sin has to be taken care of; it cannot be overlooked. God demonstrated His own righteousness by providing Jesus, a perfect, permanent and completely satisfactory sacrifice for sin. Through Jesus we can be made 'at one' with God.

Jesus was taken down from the cross and laid in a previously unused tomb. It was sealed with a huge stone placed in front of it, and guarded by soldiers. There Jesus lay for three days and two nights. On the first Easter Sunday morning, the stone rolled away, not so much to let Jesus out, but to let people look in and see that He had risen from the dead. He did what no religious or political leader or ordinary individual has ever done. He conquered death and sin by coming back to life.

The Killing Fields is an unforgettable film telling the true story of a *New York Times* reporter who was working in Cambodia and was captured by the Marxist regime, the Khmer Rouge, which was a totalitarian group known for its torturous cruelty. What this man endured while trying to find freedom is beyond belief; he was brutally beaten, imprisoned and mistreated. In his escape, he runs from one tragic situation to another. On one occasion he sinks into a bog only to discover it is a watery bog full of rotting flesh and human bones and skulls that foam to the top as he scrambles to climb out.

Having endured the rigours of the jungle while being chased by his captors, he finally steps out into a clearing and looks down. To his amazement he sees the Cambodian border, a small refugee camp, a hospital and a flag on which is a cross. At that moment the music builds to a climax, as light returns to his face, which seems to shout out, 'I'm free. I'm free!'

Jesus' work was accomplished that we might be made free. Not the freedom to do as we want, but the freedom to do what is right. He came that there might be forgiveness and new, eternal life for those who will trust Him as Lord, Saviour and Friend. We humans so often feel the need to do something to prove ourselves to God, but that is not what God wants. We need to accept within our minds and hearts the truth of God's work on our behalf, and simply receive it. Nothing more can be added to what Jesus had done on the cross for us. He alone can set us free from the slavery of following our selfish whims.

5

God wants us to know
what we must do

'To make a man happy as a lark, might be to do him grievous wrong; to make a man wake, rise, look up, turn, is worth the life and death of the Son of the Eternal.'[53] – George Mac Donald (19th century Scottish novelist and poet)

When Jesus was asked the question, 'What must we do that we may work the works of God?' He gave a startling and unexpected answer. His reply was, 'This is the work of God, that you may believe in Him whom He sent.'[54] In other words, Jesus did not speak of the good deeds we have to do, but spoke of the need for belief and trust in Him. Belief in Jesus is not the issue on which the media

---

53 *Unspoken Sermons* (Series Two), by George MacDonald, London: Longmans, Green, and Co., 1891.

54 John 6:28-29

focuses; they are concerned with whether politically we move to the left or right. There is much to strive towards, to bring justice, economic and environmental security and an end to conflict in our world, but there are also issues of eternity, of our relationship with God and of heaven and hell. These are sorted out not by striving but by receiving what God wants to give. The infinite God can fully give Himself to everyone who will ask.

The poet Louise Tarkington expressed thoughts that many have:

> I wish there were some wonderful place
> In the land of Beginning Again
> Where all our mistakes and all our heartaches
> And all our poor selfish grief
> Could be dropped like a shabby old coat at the door
> And never put on again.

God offers to a world that has lost its bearings, a completely new start. There is a new beginning for the person who will turn in repentance, and trust Christ as Lord and Saviour. The Bible says, 'Therefore, if anyone is in Christ, he is a new creation; the old has gone, the new has come!'[55] God is willing to forgive a person all that is wrong, and give to

---

55 2 Corinthians 5:17

them His righteousness, so he or she can be acceptable in His sight. Because Jesus has died and risen from the dead, we can be reconciled to His Father, God.

There was an occasion when a religious leader, called Nicodemus, came to Jesus at night time, wanting to know who Jesus really was. In the subsequent conversation, Jesus said to him, 'You must born again.'[56] We have been born once, but Jesus said we need to be born from above by the Spirit of God. It is the Holy Spirit who works in our minds to show us that we are not the people we were created to be, and then to point our attention to Jesus who loved us and gave Himself for us. God wants to work this miracle in our lives. When He does, the Holy Spirit Himself comes to live within us, and will never leave or forsake us. Our beings become God's possession, the very dwelling place of God. We can know God guiding, guarding and governing our lives through life, death and into eternity.

Anne Brontë, in her book, *The Tenant of Wildfell Hall* tells the story of Helen and the inner turmoil that she, a moral Christian woman, struggles with because of her drunken husband who is given to cruelty and immorality. Loyalty wins the day, but self-abuse takes her husband's life. His dying words to her were, 'Oh Helen, I wish you could come with me to plead for me.' Once a person has Christ

---

56 John 3:1-15

as Lord and Saviour, they have Jesus to plead their cause before the Father who is in heaven. Jesus is the mediator between God and men; He is the advocate. He is the one who will take us through life's journey, to be with Him forever. None of us is good enough for God or for heaven. Yet those who belong and have become the children of God, are promised forgiveness and eternal life with Him.

One New Year's Eve I found myself unable to sleep. About three o'clock in the morning I got out of bed and leaned against the windowsill to watch the stillness of our little cul-de-sac in the early hours of a new day. We were thick in snow, and a blizzard was still blowing. Then from the nearby woods emerged a beautiful red fox. It sniffed around a number of neighbours' gardens before wandering around ours. The next morning, I went to examine the fox tracks. To my disappointment, they had all disappeared – all covered by the fresh snow, which had continued to fall throughout the night. Musing on the incident, I couldn't help thinking that all my sins could be completely covered, never to be uncovered. It would not be snow that removed my guilt, but as the Bible puts it: 'The blood of Jesus, (God's) Son, purifies us from all sin,'[57] and 'If we confess our sins, He is faithful and

---

57 1 John 1:7

just, and will forgive us our sins and purify us from all unrighteousness.'[58]

God wants us to know how we can have the certainty that we are eternally secure with Him. It is not presumptuous to be sure of heaven. The Bible promises it to those who have come to the point when they have deliberately turned from their sin and ask Jesus Christ to be their Lord and Saviour. Here are some Bible quotations that state clearly that we can *know* we are safe in God's keeping, not because of anything we have done, but entirely because of what God has done in forgiving us and making us His children:

'Come now, let us reason together,' says the Lord, 'Though your sins are like scarlet they shall be as white as snow; though they are red as crimson, they shall be like wool.'[59]

He saved us, not because of righteous things we had done but because of His mercy. He saved us through the washing of rebirth and renewal by the Holy Spirit.[60]

---

58 1 John 1: 9

59 Isaiah 1:18

60 Titus 3:5

*For it is by grace you have been saved, through faith –
and this not from yourselves, it is the gift of God – not
by works, so that no-one can boast. For we are God's
workmanship, created in Christ Jesus to do good works,
which God prepared in advance for us to do.*[61]

*Yet all who received Him, to those who believed in His
name, He gave the right to become children of God
– children born not of natural descent, nor of human
decision or a husband's will, but born of God.*[62]

*He who has the Son has life; he who does not have the
Son of God does not have life. I write these things to you
who believe in the name of the Son of God so that you
may know that you have eternal life.*[63]

*Jesus said, 'Assuredly, I say to you, unless you are
converted and become as little children, you will by no
means enter the kingdom of heaven.'*[64]

How then is a person converted to Jesus Christ? How
does someone put his or her faith in Jesus? It is rather

---

61 Ephesians 2:8-10

62 John 1:12-13

63 1 John 5:12-13

64 Matthew 18:3 (NKJV)

like getting married. Two people, make deliberate vows to each other that forsaking all others they commit themselves to the one they love. They use simple words like 'I do' and 'I will', but those words change their whole personal standing. They then go and live out their married lives together. In a similar way, we bring words to God. We don't have to be in a church or religious setting, but need to pray to God from the heart,

- thanking God for who He is and what He has done
- confessing to Him our sin and asking Him for forgiveness, because of Jesus' death and resurrection
- asking Him, by His Holy Spirit, to come to live within our life as Lord and Friend.

God hears such a prayer, and promises to answer: as we read that 'whoever calls on the name of the Lord will be saved.'[65] When God has gone to such great lengths to reach and rescue us, it is right that we should respond to His love by receiving Him, and all He has to give. Many have found it very helpful to express their faith and commitment using a prayer with words like these:

---

65 Romans 10:13

Dear God, Thank you that you have revealed Yourself to this world. Thank You for giving me life, and for showing yourself to me. I confess to you all my sin, and with Your help I want to turn from it. I ask, that because of Jesus, you would forgive me. I want Him to become my Lord, my Saviour and Friend forever. Help me to follow You and grow to become a strong Christian. Thank you for loving me, and hearing this prayer, which I pray in the name of Jesus. Amen.

It really is important to come to the moment in life where one turns to God from living one's own sinful, selfish life. The Bible calls this turning from sin, repentance.

It is crucial to trust Jesus in order to receive forgiveness and a new life, with Him as Lord and Saviour. The Bible calls that trust, believing, or faith.

In the Old Testament, there is a beautiful little love song, called the Song of Solomon which describes the relationship between a man and his lover. It shows how God made us man and woman, and how He honours love and sex. But there is a sad scene in the book where the girl has gone to her room for the night. She has anointed herself with perfumes, and retired to her bed. Then there is a knock at her door; she knows that her lover has arrived. Though she wants to be with him, she hesitates, and doesn't respond. She muses on the thought that she has now gone to bed, and she doesn't want to get up. Then, suddenly, he leaves, and cannot be found. She realises that all the perfume is absolutely worthless now the lover has gone.

It would be sad, if in a similar way, when God has revealed Himself to us, knocking on the door of our lives, he should be ignored or shunned. The obvious response is to invite Him into our lives, to trust Him and enjoy Him forever.

When one truly trusts God in this way it is the beginning of a whole new life. It is the new birth Jesus spoke about. God takes us at our word, and gives His word that we will be accepted in Christ. We are then at the start of the whole new adventure of living life with and for the Lord Jesus. God, by His Holy Spirit, comes to live within us, so that we become the dwelling place of God. It is amazing that God cleans us up by forgiving us, and giving us Himself. He will never leave, but will take us through life's journey to be with Himself forever. Carefully read these words from the Bible. They were written in the first century to encourage Christians living in the heart of the Roman Empire, which was so antagonistic to the Christian message:

If God is for us, who can be against us? He who did not spare His own Son, but gave Him up for us all – how will He not also, along with Him, graciously give us all things? Who will bring any charge against those whom God has chosen? It is God who justifies. Who is he that condemns? Christ Jesus, who died – more than that, who was raised to life – is at the right hand of God, and is also interceding for us. Who shall separate us from the love of Christ? Shall trouble or hardship or persecution or famine or nakedness or danger or sword? As it is written:

'For your sake we face death all day long;
we are considered as sheep to be slaughtered.'

No, in all these things we are more than conquerors through Him who loved us. For I am convinced that neither death nor life, neither angels nor demons, neither the present nor the future, nor any powers, neither height nor depth, nor anything else in all creation, will be able to separate us from the love of God that is in Christ Jesus our Lord.[66]

God has given us help so that we can start to grow in our faith and knowledge of God. The Holy Spirit, now living within us, will give us the strength to start living as we should. We know what that is by reading the Bible, which

---

66 Romans 8:31-39

is God's word to us, in written form. I recommend the habit of spending some time with God each day, preferably without any exceptions. Let it become a daily, dogged, delightful discipline to set aside time each day to read God's word, and enjoy your relationship with God. Start by working through the New Testament. If you can buy a modern version of the Bible, whose print is not too small, it definitely helps! Don't worry if you don't understand everything. God will speak through His written word, to you. He will give you the desire and power to do all that He commands.

There are also some very helpful Bible aids to help you in your reading.[67] You will find that the Bible will become quite exciting to read, as you learn what God has said, and how different it often is to the agenda that the world is obsessed with. One man, centuries ago said, 'My greatest delight is to be in a nook, with the Book!'

Just as you listen to God speaking and teaching you, through reading the Bible, you can speak to Him by praying. Learn to thank and praise Him. The great scientist, Sir Isaac Newton, said, 'I can take my telescope

---

67 *Our Daily Bread*, with daily readings and notes, is available from Radio Bible Class, Box 1, Carnforth, Lancashire, LA5 9ES, England. *Explore* is a quarterly book of Bible reading notes available from The Good Book Company; email: admin@thegoodbook.co.uk. To really dig into the whole Bible over three years, I recommend *Search the Scriptures*, edited by Alan M. Stibbs, published by IVP.

and look millions of miles into space; but I can go away to my room, and in prayer get nearer to God and heaven than I can when assisted by all the telescopes of earth.' Reading the Psalms in the Bible can help us in knowing how to praise God. Confess your sins to Him. Simply because you have become a Christian doesn't mean that you will be temptation-free or perfect overnight! Every Christian struggles against real temptations to do wrong. We are reminded that the things which satisfy our wrong desires, and the pleasures of this world, pass away, but that the person who does the will of God lives forever.[68] You can pray for others: your family, friends, Church, government, world situations, etc.

As well, God invites you to ask Him to help, guide and use you. Jesus said, 'Come to Me, all you who are weary and burdened, and I will give you rest. Take my yoke upon you and learn from Me, for I am gentle and humble in heart, and you will find rest for your souls. For My yoke is easy and My burden is light.'[69]

Church is a great place to start to grow in your Christian faith. When you become a child of God, you become part of His family. Church is where you can share worship, serve God, and witness to your faith with fellow believers.

---

68 1 John 2:15-17

69 Matthew 11:28-30

Of course, no church is perfect, for it is a collection of sinners who are gathering together. However, it is vital that you make sure your church is one where the Bible is believed and preached; where Jesus is the focus, and is loved and served; and where there are people who will care for you spiritually, and with whom you can tell others the good news of Jesus.

Sharing with others, who God is and what He has done for us, is a way in which we can show that we love God and want others to know Him too. Ask God to give you the courage to tell those you know or meet about Him. You don't need to be an oddball to winsomely share the most wonderful relationship you have with God, through Jesus.

None of these things make us Christians, or earn us favour with God. Rather, they grow out of love for God after all He has done for us. We demonstrate that we love God by the things we do, but we enter into an eternal relationship with God, through what He has done.

God wants us to know this. And He wants everyone else to know it too!

Acknowledgements

When I first understood that God had taken the initiative to reach out not only to the world, but to me, I was overjoyed. At last, God began to make sense to me, and I responded to His love, shown in Jesus, by trusting Him as Lord and Saviour. I have not regretted that moment: God has never been a disappointment. I pray that this little book will make this wonderful truth clear to you, too.

I want to thank my mother, now in her late eighties, but whose eye for detail is undimmed. Good grammar and the comma owe their continuing existence to her. Thanks too to Emma Balch who, living in Buenos Aires, scrutinised this manuscript, and improved it.

This book is dedicated to

Warren and Betty Wiersbe

American author and pastor, and his wife, who first encouraged me to write, and have been faithful friends, lavishing pastoral care, friendship and cheer in my direction for many years. Their love for God, and glint in their eye, demonstrate the value of listening to the things God wants us to know.

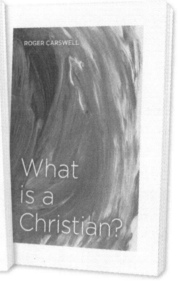